G000164553

THE WISDOM
OF
SAINT PATRICK

THE WISDOM
OF
SAINT PATRICK

Compiled and introduced by Justin Butcher

LION
Giftlines

This edition copyright © 2000 Lion Publishing

Published by
Lion Publishing plc
Sandy Lane West, Oxford, England
www.lion-publishing.co.uk
ISBN 0 7459 4400 0

First edition 2000
10 9 8 7 6 5 4 3 2 1 0

A catalogue record for this book is available
from the British Library

Typeset in 12/13 Venetian 301
Printed and bound in Singapore

CONTENTS

INTRODUCTION

The son of Romano-British parents, Patrick was born around AD 385 at Bannavem Taberniae, somewhere on the west coast of Wales or northern England. Both his father and grandfather were ordained clergy in the local church.

At sixteen, Patrick was abducted by Irish raiders and carried off to work as slave-herdsman for a chieftain in County Antrim. Looking back on the anguish of this period of exile, he speaks of it as his doorway into the spiritual life, through which he first began to encounter God as his *anam-cara*, his soul-friend.

After six years of slavery, he had a dream in which he saw a ship waiting to carry him home. He managed to escape, and after a journey of some two hundred miles across Ireland on foot, he found the very ship just as it was about to embark for Britain.

After further adventures, he returned joyfully to his family, burning with a desire to study for the priesthood. He went to train under Germanus at Auxerre in Gaul. It was there that an angel appeared to him in a dream bearing letters from Ireland. As he began to read, Patrick heard the voice of the Irish calling him to 'return and walk once more among us'.

Patrick completed his training and was appointed priest and then bishop. He returned to Ireland around 432, landing at Strangford Lough. Over the next thirty years he carried out an extraordinarily zealous and demanding mission of preaching, baptizing and ordaining throughout the length and breadth of Ireland. He endured tremendous hardships, often coming into violent conflict with pagan druids, hostile chieftains and murderous kings. Nevertheless, he succeeded in converting thousands to faith in Christ.

The passages in this book have been drawn almost exclusively from the two surviving works by his own hand: his *Confession* and his letter to the

British prince Coroticus. These excerpts vividly demonstrate his passionate devotion to the Irish people, his fervent love of God's creation, his uncompromising thirst for the truth and his sensitivity to the world of dreams and visions.

There are many colourful legends about Patrick. Whether or not we believe that he banished snakes, battled with druids in contests of wizardry at the court of the High King at Tara or haggled with angels for forty days and nights on the Croagh Patrick in County Mayo, one thing is certain: without Patrick the Christian faith would have vanished from the British Isles.

By his death in 461, Christianity in Western Europe had virtually been extinguished by pagan invaders from the north. However, in Ireland there was a flourishing church with deep roots, due in no small part to the work of Patrick, who may justly be called the father of Celtic Christianity.

JUSTIN BUTCHER

THE WAY
OF CHRIST

CHRIST'S INCARNATION

I arise today
Strengthened by Christ's own baptism,
Made strong by his crucifixion and burial,
Made strong by his resurrection
and his ascension,
Made strong by his descent to meet me
on the day of doom.

The 'Deer's Cry' from the Breastplate (Lorica) of St Patrick, circa 700

THE GREAT STONE

I was like a great stone
Lying deep in mud,
Until he who is in power came
And in his mercy
Lifted me up.
Yes, that is how it was,
He did indeed raise me up,
For he placed me
On the very top of the wall.

And so, because of that,
I must shout out loud to the Lord
In order to give back
Some small thing
For all his gifts that are so great
Both here and in eternity.

The mere mind of man
Can never plumb
Such gifts as these.

Confession, I:12

3
FISH WELL

It is our duty to fish well
And with loving care,
Just as the Lord urges and teaches us:
Come after me, and I
Will make you fishers of men.
And again, he says through the prophets,
Look, I send fishers and many hunters,
Says God, and so forth.
Because of this,
It was vital
That we let down our nets,
So that a vast crowd and multitude
Might be taken for God.

Confession, IV:40

FORGIVE EVERYONE

To forgive everyone
Who has done us evil,
In voice, in word, in deed,
Is the command of the king of heaven.

To love those who hate us
In this earthly world;
To do good to those who persecute us
Is the command of God.

From the Rule of St Carthage, circa 800*

* St Carthage (died 636), founder of the famous monastery of Lismore,
County Waterford, was the first Celtic monk to write extensively about the
duties of anamchairdeas or soul-friendship: a constant theme in St Patrick's
writings and a primary feature of the early Celtic church in Ireland.

SATAN TEMPTED ME

As I lay sleeping,
Satan tempted me full sorely.
The memory will go with me
As long as I stay in this body.
He fell right over me, like a huge rock,
So that none of my limbs
Had any strength left in them.
How did I know
In my ignorant spirit
To cry out to Elijah by name?

And while all this befell me,
I saw the sun rise in the sky,
But still I called unceasingly Elijah, Elijah!
With all the strength I had.

And suddenly, the splendour of that sun
Flooded over me, and at once
I was rid of my powerlessness.
I fully believe that it was Christ my Lord
Who came to my aid.

Confession, II:20

A SLAVE IN CHRIST

By descent I was a freeman,
Born of a decurion father;
Yet I have sold this nobility of mine.
I am not ashamed,
Nor do I regret
That it might have meant
Some advantage to others;
In short, I am a slave in Christ
To this faraway people
For the indescribable glory
Of everlasting life
Which is in Jesus Christ our Lord.

Letter to Coroticus, III:10

ANGELS,
SAINTS AND
MARTYRS

THE HEAVENLY HOST

I arise today
Strengthened by cherubims' love of God,
By obedience of all angels,
By service of archangels,
By hope in reward of my resurrection,
By prayers of the fathers,
By predictions of prophets,
By preachings of apostles,
By the faith of confessors,
By the shyness of holy virgins,
By deeds of all holy men.

From the 'Deer's Cry'

SOUL-FRIENDSHIP

If you be anybody's soul-friend,
Do not sell his soul.
Do not be a blind man leading the blind.
Do not allow him to fall into neglect.

From the Rule of St Carthage

LAMENT FOR CHRISTIAN MARTYRS

I do not know what I shall say
or how I may speak any more
Of those who are dead of these children of God,
Whom the sword has struck down so harshly,
beyond all belief.

For it is written, Weep with those who weep.

Because of all this, my voice is raised
in sorrow and mourning.
O my most beautiful, my lovely brethren
And my sons whom I begot in Christ,
I have lost count of your number.
What can I do to help you now?

How I mourn for you, who are so very dear to me!

If this wicked deed, so horrible, so unutterable,
Had to happen,
Thanks be to God — as men, believing and baptized,
You have left this world behind for Paradise.

There your hearts will leap,
like calves let free from the tether.

Adapted from the Letter to Coroticus, III and IV

DELIVER ME, O JESUS

Deliver me, O Jesus,
as thou didst deliver Eli and Enoch.
Deliver me as thou didst deliver Noah
from the flood.
Deliver me as thou didst deliver Abraham
from the hands of the Chaldeans.
Deliver me as thou didst deliver Lot
from the sin of the cities.

Save me, O Jesus
whom thy mother's kin rejected,
As thou didst save Jacob
from his brother's hands.
Save me from the cause of every disease
As thou didst save Job
from the devil's tribulations.

Save me as thou didst save Patrick
from the poison at Tara.

From the Martyrology of Tallaght by Oengus the Culdee, circa 797

IF THIS SHOULD BE MY LOT

Even if my body were to remain unburied,
Or my corpse be torn pitifully
limb from limb
By dogs or wild beasts,
Or that birds of the air eat it up,
I know with utter certainty,
If this should be my lot,
That I shall have gained my soul
As well as my body,
Because without shadow of doubt
On that last day we shall all rise again
In the sun's own brilliant blaze,
That is, in the glory of Christ Jesus
Our Redeemer.

Confession, V:59

CREATION

RUNE OF ST PATRICK

At Tara today in this fateful hour
I place all heaven with its power,
And the sun with its brightness,
And the snow with its whiteness,
And fire with all the strength it hath,
And lightning with its rapid wrath,
And the winds with their swiftness
along the path,
And the sea with its deepness,
And the rocks with their steepness,
And the earth with its starkness:
All these I place
By God's almighty help and grace,
Between myself and the powers of darkness.

From the 'Deer's Cry'

PRAYER OF THE ELEMENTS

Although I might be staying in a forest
Or out on a mountainside,
It would be the same;
Even before dawn broke,
I would be aroused to pray.
In snow, in frost, in rain,
I scarcely heeded any discomfort,
Never slack, always full of zest.
It is clear to me now,
This was due to the fervour
Of the Spirit within me.

Confession, II:16

GOD OF ALL THINGS

Our God, God of all men,
God of heaven and earth, seas and rivers,
God of sun and moon, of all the stars,
God of high mountain and lowly valleys,
God over heaven, and in heaven,
and under heaven.
He has a dwelling in heaven and earth and sea
And in all things that are in them.

Attributed to St Patrick

15
ARMAGH

It is Armagh that I love,
A deep thorpe,
A dear hill,
A fortress
Which my soul haunts.

Attributed to St Patrick

ALMIGHTY
PROTECTOR

GOD MY GUIDE

I arise today
With God's strength to pilot me,
God's might to uphold me,
God's wisdom to guide me,
God's eye to look ahead for me,
God's ear to hear me,
God's word to speak for me,
God's hand to defend me,
God's way to lie before me,
God's shield to protect me,
God's host to safeguard me.

From the 'Deer's Cry'

POWERS OF DARKNESS

Against devils' traps,
Against attraction of sin,
Against pull of nature,
Against all who wish me ill,
Near and far, alone and in a crowd

I summon all God's powers to protect me

Against every cruel and wicked power
That stands against me, body and soul,
Against false prophets' wild words,
Against dark ways of heathen,
Against false laws of heretics,
Against magic and idolatry,
Against spells of smiths, witches and wizards,
Against every false lore
That snares body and soul.

Christ protect me today
Against poison, against burning,
Against drowning, against wounding,
So that I may come
To enjoy your rich reward.

From the 'Deer's Cry'

WHATEVER WILL COME MY WAY

Whatever will come my way,
Whether good or bad,
I may accept it calmly,
And always give thanks to God,
Who has ever shown me
How I should believe in him
Unfailing without end.
And he has heard and helped me,
So that I, for all my ignorance,
Should in these latter days
Dare to undertake this work
That is so holy and wonderful.

Confession, III:34

WHAT I FEAR

What I fear most is to lose
The labour I have begun,
And not I alone,
But Christ the Lord,
Who bade me come here
And be with my flock
For the rest of my life,
If the Lord so desires.
And he will shield me
From every evil,
So that I do no sin in his sight.

Confession, IV:43

ALL-POWERFUL GOD

As every day arrives, I expect
Either sudden death or deception
Or being taken back as a slave
Or some such other misfortune.
But I fear none of these,
Since I look to the promises of heaven
And have flung myself into the hands
Of the all-powerful God,
Who rules as Lord everywhere.

Confession, V:55

THE GIFT OF GOD

But still, I may not hide
The gift of God,
Which he so generously gave us
In the land of my captivity.
Because then I sought him
With such a will
And there I found him.
And he kept me safe from all evils,
By means of his indwelling Spirit,
So I believe,
Who has continued his working within me
Up to this present day.

Confession, III:33

THE
INNER REALM

THE CAIM* OF CHRIST'S PRESENCE

Christ ever with me,
Christ before me, Christ behind me,
Christ within me,
Christ beneath me, Christ above me,
Christ to my right side, Christ to my left,
Christ in his breadth, Christ in his length,
Christ in his depth,
Christ in the heart of every man
who thinks of me,
Christ in the mouth of every man
who speaks to me,
Christ in every eye that sees me,
Christ in every ear that hears me.

From the 'Deer's Cry'

* A caim in the Celtic custom is an encompassing prayer, invoking the
protection of God on all sides. The person praying would traditionally
extend the index finger of the right hand and draw an imaginary circle
around themselves as they prayed.

My Enemy the Flesh

My enemy the flesh
Continually drags me
Down to death –
Indulgence in illicit pleasures.
And I well know in part
Why I have not led a perfect life,
Just like other believers,
But still I confess my Lord,
And I do not blush for shame
In his sight.

Confession, IV:44

My Soul's Origin

I am certain
In my heart
That all that I am
I have received
From God.

Letter to Coroticus, I:1

I Saw Him Praying

I saw him praying within my soul;
It seemed as if I was still inside my body,
And then I heard him above me,
Over the inner man.
There he was, praying with many a groan,
And as these things befell me, I was amazed
And kept marvelling and wondering
Who he might be,
Who was praying in this wise within me.
But as this prayer was ending,
He declared that it was the Spirit.

Confession, II:25

HONOUR THAT LASTS

The only honour that lasts
Is what is firmly felt in the heart.

Confession, V:54

STRONG
NAME OF THE
TRINITY

A MIGHTY STRENGTH

I arise today
In mighty strength,
Making in my mouth the Trinity,
Believing in mind three Persons,
Confessing in heart they are one,
Thanking my Creator.

Salvation is from the Lord,
Salvation is from the Lord,
Salvation is from Christ.
May your salvation,
Three Lords,
Be always with us.

From the 'Deer's Cry'

THREE FOLDS OF THE CLOTH

Three folds of the cloth,
yet only one napkin is there,
Three joints in the finger,
but still only one finger fair;
Three leaves of the shamrock,
yet no more than one shamrock to wear,
Frost, snowflakes and ice,
all in water their origin share,
Three Persons in God;
to one God alone we make prayer.

Traditional Celtic

Not Separate Are They

He inspires all things, he quickens all things.
He is over all things, he supports all things.

He makes the light of the sun to shine,
He surrounds the moon and the stars,
He has made wells in the arid earth,
Placed dry islands in the sea.

He has a Son co-eternal with himself
And the Holy Spirit breathes in them;
Not separate are the Father and the Son
and the Holy Spirit.

Attributed to St Patrick

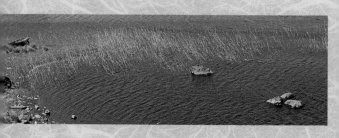